IT'S **NOT** MAGIC

SECRETS OF PERFORMING AT YOUR BEST

MIKE TOY

Dee Ann—
Loved "It's My Pleasure"
Can't wait to read "Bet on Talent"
God bless!
Mike Toy
11/14/19

INDIE BOOKS
INTERNATIONAL

It's Not Magic
Secrets of Performing at Your Best
Mike Toy

Published by:
Indie Books International LLC
2424 Vista Way #316
Oceanside, CA 92054

Copyright © MMXVII by Mike Toy

ISBN-10: 1-941870-86-4
ISBN-13: 978-1-941870-86-0
Library of Congress Control Number: 2017937103

Praise for *It's Not Magic*

"There's nothing more important than human connection. Mike Toy's book will help you to build more connection and be more influential. Maybe it is magic."

TIM DAVID, AUTHOR OF *MAGIC WORDS: THE SCIENCE AND SECRETS BEHIND SEVEN WORDS THAT MOTIVATE, ENGAGE, AND INFLUENCE*

"This fascinating book shows you a variety of methods and techniques you can use to be more persuasive and entertaining with everyone you meet."

BRIAN TRACY, AUTHOR AND SPEAKER

"Mike Toy's people skills tips will help you better get along with others. He writes with a light touch and a spirit of service that make it a fun and easy read."

DANIEL H. PINK, AUTHOR OF *TO SELL IS HUMAN AND DRIVE*

"Fun and full of insights. Mike's secrets will up your game and increase your value to everyone around you."

JONAH BURGER, AUTHOR OF *INVISIBLE INFLUENCE*

"The most important skill in the world a person can possess is having the ability to build rapport and strong relationships. Toy shows you how to do just that in this book, with easy yet effective ways that you can improve the quality of your life and more importantly other people's lives."

JOHN R. DiJULIUS III, AUTHOR OF *THE CUSTOMER SERVICE REVOLUTION*

"Mike has a way with words. His advice will jump off the page and energize you and your relationships."

JON GORDON, AUTHOR OF *THE ENERGY BUS* AND *THE CARPENTER*

"People are now looking for short reads with great impact —Mike Toy has achieved this. Great communications skills can create magic in your life. *It's Not Magic* will show you how."

JOSEPH SHERREN, AUTHOR OF *iLEAD*

"Engaging people is an art. Mike Toy offers the tips and tricks to engage people in this easy to read book."

DEBRA FINE, AUTHOR OF *THE FINE ART OF SMALL TALK*

"From standing out to fear of failure to dealing with difficult people, Mike Toy's new book lays out new formulas and frameworks for you to transform your own personal impact and influence. This book is magical advice you need!"

NICK WESTERGAARD, AUTHOR OF *GET SCRAPPY: SMARTER DIGITAL MARKETING FOR BUSINESSES BIG AND SMALL*

"Mike Toy offers pragmatic, useful advice that is fun to read. If your work involves other people (and all work does), you need this book!"

PAMELA SLIM, AUTHOR OF *ESCAPE FROM CUBICLE NATION* AND *BODY OF WORK*

"*It's Not Magic* is a fascinating book. As a speaking and communications expert the techniques all made perfect sense to me. Delivered from the point of view of a professional *magician gave the information a new twist. There's no sleight-of-hand needed to get the results you want."*

PATRICIA FRIPP, PAST PRESIDENT, NATIONAL SPEAKERS ASSOCIATION

"As a former magician myself, Mike has even wowed me with his expert prestidigitation skills. Now, he hits the spot in his new book where he teaches readers the magical secrets of communication and engaging others."

JUDY CARTER, AUTHOR OF *THE COMEDY BIBLE*

"I picked up a book on magic and got secrets on how to get unstuck. The real magic in this book are the life lessons you will learn. And Mike reveals how these magic life lessons are done. No secrets. It's a quick and easy read. I highly recommend it."

ED TATE, CSP – CERTIFIED SPEAKING PROFESSIONAL, WORLD CHAMPION OF PUBLIC SPEAKING

"Mike Toy shares lessons from the entertainment stage in this thoughtful and engaging book. It's Not Magic, actually is magic as well as an approachable journey into the essence of interpersonal excellence Buy it now and voila success will appear."

JOSEPH MICHELLI, AUTHOR OF *DRIVEN TO DELIGHT*, *THE NEW GOLD STANDARD*, *THE STARBUCKS EXPERIENCE* AND *THE ZAPPOS EXPERIENCE*

"Mike Toy shows you how to use everything up your sleeve to connect with people around you."

DAVID MEERMAN SCOTT, AUTHOR OF *THE NEW RULES OF MARKETING*

"Mike is a people person and his book is jam-packed with practical advice and easy ways of how to become one yourself, even if you're an introvert. There's something in here for everyone."

ALEXANDRA WATKINS, AUTHOR OF *HELLO, MY NAME IS AWESOME*

"Mike has a keen understanding of people and in this book, he offers up terrific tips for optimizing your interactions with everyone from clients to co-workers to friends and family."

KEN DYCHTWALD, PhD, PRESIDENT AND CEO OF AGE WAVE

"A fun and quick read that will remind you of the easily forgotten (yet vital) basics of connecting with people. What could be more important in life?"

VERNE HARNISH, AUTHOR OF *SCALING UP (ROCKEFELLER HABITS 2.0)*

"Mike Toy is a comedy magician who knows how to connect with an audience. In this book he shows how many of the same skills performers use to connect with a room full of people apply to our one-on-one interactions on any given day. People skills aren't magic, but they're incredibly powerful when used effectively. This book offers tips to tap into that power."

DAVID DISALVO, AUTHOR OF *WHAT MAKES YOUR BRAIN HAPPY AND WHY YOU SHOULD DO THE OPPOSITE*

"Simple, powerful life lessons told through the relatable wonder of magic. Highly recommended!"

JAY BAER, PRESIDENT OF CONVINCE & CONVERT AND AUTHOR OF *HUG YOUR HATERS*

"Read this book and your success will appear to you as if pulled from a magic hat."

JEFFREY HAYZLETT, PRIMETIME TV AND PODCAST HOST, CHAIRMAN C-SUITE NETWORK

"Wouldn't it be great if you can wave a magic wand and all your relationships improved just like that? Mike's insights will you the edge to be unforgettable and well-liked, both in your personal and business life."

FORD SAEKS, CEO OF PRIME CONCEPTS GROUP

"Full of real life observations and applications. Mike's insights really hit home."

DR. TONY ALESSANDRA, AUTHOR OF *THE PLATINUM RULE*

"Great insights delivered through this interesting metaphor! Well done, Mike Toy. You make it simple and keep it fun."

DARREN LACROIX, CSP – CERTIFIED SPEAKING PROFESSIONAL, AS, WORLD CHAMPION SPEAKER

"Magic is about tension, the difference between what we think we see and reality. Mike puts that tension to good work to give us dozens of new ways to think about our work."

SETH GODIN, AUTHOR OF *LINCHPIN*

"Practical. Wise. Actionable steps. What more can you ask for?"

CRAIG VALENTINE, WORLD CHAMPION SPEAKER

"It's not an illusion. This book is real. Mike Toy is the Houdini of professional development."

ANDREW DAVIS, AUTHOR OF *BRANDSCAPING* AND *TOWN INC.*

"A trove of solid life advice that's easy and fun to dip into. I just don't know how he got it all into that little silk hat."

CATHERINE NOMURA, CO-AUTHOR OF INTERNATIONAL BESTSELLER, *THE LAWS OF LIFETIME GROWTH*

"Mike Toy is a man after my own heart—a nice guy with a positive attitude who wants to make a difference in people's lives. This little book will tell you all you need to know to get through your days with a smile on your face. Read it and discover the magic in your life!"

KEN BLANCHARD, CO-AUTHOR OF *THE NEW ONE MINUTE MANAGER*® AND *ONE MINUTE MENTORING*

"A magical piece of work. Apply its truths and you'll be better for it and everyone else around you, too."

MARSHALL GOLDSMITH, AUTHOR OF THE #1 *NEW YORK TIMES* BESTSELLER, *TRIGGERS*

For Walter Henrichsen

My Friend and Mentor

Table of Contents

Foreword

In your hands you hold a magical book written by a spirited performer. Mike Toy is rare indeed. In fact, his down-to-earth and quiet confidence is captivating. We live in a world of challenge and change. No matter what season of your career you are living, you now have a guiding set of principles that can lead your way through the ups and downs of workplace productivity.

Mike has given you the keys to raising the bar on your future performance. Let today be the dividing line in the sand and you will create a new chapter of ideas, goals, milestones, and moments that matter.

Regardless of what has gone before you, you can unlock a new combination for your career on purpose and by design, not by accident. It will require serious reflection and heavy lifting. You will have new results to celebrate and the rewards will be priceless.

Always remember, no change—no change.

After reading Mike's book, answering questions and

coming up with new answers, your life will never be the same. In fact, keep his book handy and reread over and over. Make it your desktop or bedside companion and it will serve you well. Refer to it often and it will keep you on path or help you get back on plan if you go off on a tangent disguised as an opportunity.

One wish I have for you is to hear Mike speak. You will meet a force for good in this world. You will learn and laugh out loud in his presentations. I am fortunate to call Mike my friend.

I leave you with a single word. It is my gift to you and represents so much of what I have learned and been reminded of in this special book. It is Latin for, "Keep going." I want you to remember this word for the rest of your life. And, you will be a better person, employee, manager, leader, and friend.

Ultreia!

Mark LeBlanc

Speaker, pilgrim and author of *Never Be the Same* and *Growing Your Business*

Preface

Why I'm Writing This Book

For many years, I've been performing as a comedy magician on stage, making thousands of people laugh until it hurts. I admit that I'm not the best magician in the world.

There are many who have better finger skills and sleight-of-hand. To compensate, I tap into my personality. I engage with my audiences and people laugh with me as if I was their best friend while I pickpocket their watches, wallets, and even their ties. Comedy is my best misdirection.

I use every people skill I know to my advantage: tone of voice, volume, eye contact, physical motion, facial expressions, and so forth. Over the years, I've learned a lot about what makes people like you and am excited to share these insights.

Other insights come from seeing conflicts between people, asking why they happen, and coming up with solutions to solve them. I've learned from people all around me, from both good and bad examples.

There are instruction manuals for just about anything you buy, be it a dishwasher, a TV, a car, you name it. But when it comes to life, no one was born with an instruction manual. A huge part of how we relate with people comes from our influences as children. It does make a difference how we were parented: whether we felt loved and cared for, how others treated us. This even affects how we view ourselves, our social confidence, and how we view others.

Let me tell you my story. I grew up in San Francisco, California, as a third-generation Chinese-American. My dad had a rough childhood. When he was a kid, he was rejected by his peers and didn't find love at home. His dad verbally and physically abused him. It got so bad that he even ran away from San Francisco, all the way to New York City. I can understand why he is the way he is today. He doesn't have any friends. He doesn't have anyone to listen to him. And he keeps people a football field away. When people try to reach out to him, he puts them down, essentially preventing anyone from getting close.

Obviously, growing up with such a father had a tremendous effect on me. I never felt close to him. I didn't want to invite friends over to the house because he would embarrass me. I didn't feel comfortable sharing any problems in school because I knew he couldn't empathize. And I wasn't sure what to do about all this. So even though he was physically present, he was emotionally missing.

Fortunately for me, there were people along the way who picked up where my father lacked and played key roles in helping me develop people skills. Among them were teachers, relatives, family friends, and my mother. From these wonderful people I learned, often through trial and error, how to relate to people. This includes how to talk to people, how to show appreciation, how to be liked, and so on.

My goal in writing this book is to help you develop people skills so you can better relate and serve the people around you. I'm honored to share these insights and stories with you.

Yours,

Mike Toy

To receive my e-newsletters visit:

www.itsnotmagicbook.com

To inquire about my availability for speaking or training contact me at www.mikejtoy.com

Why You Should Try to Be Well Liked

The Secret to Magic in Your Life

"Sometimes magic is just someone spending more time on something than anyone else might reasonably expect."

—TELLER

This could easily have been the book title. After all, that's the end goal of having amazing people skills. The truth is that no matter how good you are at being liked, there will always be some people who will not like you. Maybe they're jealous of you. Maybe they don't agree with your views on a topic. Maybe you have a quirk that rubs them the wrong way. You can't please everyone, and you shouldn't try. Just accept that there will be some who don't like you. At the end of the day, you need to be true to yourself.

A lot of what I learned about people skills, I learned in high school. I knew as a freshman that I wanted to become the student body president. I had to wait until the end of my junior year to run. But I had a head start. I knew that popularity wins elections. I had to be more liked than the people I ran against.

So I did everything I knew to be liked by others. I gave Christmas gifts to teachers. They would praise me before their classes. I remembered people's birthdays. I socialized and chatted with people who were less-than-cool. The school basketball team couldn't get enough of my humor. I helped people with their homework assignments. I was friends with everybody; even the custodians liked me. Well, the plan worked. When it came time for people to vote, they voted me in.

"I just got promoted again.
It's easy to succeed if everyone likes you!"

The rest of life is similar to high school. People who are liked have advantages over those who aren't. The benefits of being well liked include:

- Others wanting to help you

- Others caring about you

- More likely to get invited to social events

- No shortage of people who want to be your friend

- More likely to get hired

- More likely to get promoted

- People are more likely to do business with you

- You'll have a happier life

Ready for more? Then let's get started!

How to Make Self-Defeating Thoughts Disappear

David Copperfield and the Statue of Liberty

*The first magician I ever saw was David Copperfield.
I was glued to the TV. What was he going to do next?
After a few gestures the curtains dropped and the
Statue of Liberty was gone.*

Have you ever wished it was that easy to make bad things disappear?

Have you ever put something off because you thought it was either too hard, too challenging, or too demanding? But once you did it, you realized that it wasn't so bad after all and that what was preventing you from doing it was all in your head?

For the life of me, I've always thought that I couldn't do any car maintenance like changing a battery. I made so many excuses: "What if I do it wrong and mess up the whole car?" "What if I get electrocuted and die?" "I'm not a mechanic, for crying out loud."

Well, last time, I didn't feel like paying someone to change my battery, so I decided to look up online videos on how to do it. After messing around for forty-five minutes, I figured it out.

I realized that what had been stopping me from doing this before were my doubts, fear, and uneasiness with something new. It wasn't because I didn't have the ability.

In other words, it was all in my head: a self-defeating thought.

Mental roadblocks come in all sizes and shapes. It could be a loss of self-confidence because a professor didn't believe you were capable. Or a parent who only criticized you; you lived in fear of disappointing him or her, so you never try new things. Or maybe you think the job you have now is as good a career as you can ever get so you don't venture anywhere else.

What are your self-defeating thoughts? What's holding you back from achieving greater things? Figure them out and challenge them!

For the top three most common self-limiting beliefs that you don't even know you have that's affecting your influence abilities and how to overcome them download it here: www.itsnotmagicbook.com/self-limiting

How to Get Others to Be Interested in You

Chinese Linking Rings

One of the classics of magic is the Chinese linking rings, in which a magician makes two seemingly solid rings link and unlink from each other at will. What makes the magic even stronger is when there's a story behind it. Each ring is like a circle of life. When we're genuinely interested in others we're mysteriously linked.

Meet my friend Gary. He is, let's just say, a big guy. Four-hundred pounds big and an average-looking guy. Not super rich. But what you don't know about him just by looking at him is that his wife is a former Miss Missouri. On the face of it, it just doesn't make any sense: why would a Miss Missouri marry *him?* So I asked him about it.

Gary told me, "A lot of guys who want to attract an amazingly beautiful woman are going about it the wrong way. They ask the question, 'How can I look more like Brad Pitt?' Well, the truth is, you can't! The secret to getting my wife to notice me was how I made our conversations all about her."

Gary was genuinely interested in her and her well-being. He remembered small details in early conversations and asked about them in subsequent conversations. Slowly, Miss Missouri fell in love with him because of how he made her feel.

People care about people who are genuinely interested in them, not for what they can get out of them. The more they perceive your genuine care for them, the more open they will be to develop a relationship with you. Do you want people to care about your needs and wants? Then care about them...*first.* Be interested in others and they'll be interested in you.

How to Show Interest in What Interests Others

Magician Patter

Part of any magician's act is "patter," or what we say while we're performing tricks. A comedy magician has to incorporate jokes into the magic in addition to typical patter like "Pick a card, any card, do not let me see the card." A longstanding magician's joke used with audience volunteers is, "What's your name? Tricia? Can I call you Tricia? **When** *can I call you, Tricia?" Patter is the backbone of connecting with an audience. Connecting one-on-one begins with finding common interests.*

To connect with people, find out what interests them. Ask, "So, what do you like doing for fun?" Now, sometimes what interests them won't interest you. Maybe the other person is into running marathons and you're not. Or maybe the other person loves cats and you don't. Just because someone is really fascinated with rocks doesn't mean you need to get a Ph.D. in geology to connect. Of course, the level of your interest can vary.

Finding common ground, even with a rock enthusiast, simply requires you to ask questions like, "So how do you know how old a rock is?" "What do you think is inside the earth?" People love talking about their favorite topics. They are always looking for a listening ear. And when you take an interest in them, they'll take an interest in you. From there on out, you can segue to any other topic. That's how connections are formed.

Another way to show interest is simply to be observant of anything obvious that might have a special meaning to a person. For example, if someone is wearing a bracelet, ask, "So what's the story behind the bracelet?" Or if someone is wearing a sports logo t-shirt, ask, "How long have you been a [fill-in-the-blank] fan?" Or just ask, "What kind of things are you passionate about?"

5

MAGICAL INSPIRATION

"We are all capable of infinitely more than we believe. We are stronger and more resourceful than we know, and we can endure much more than we think we can."

—DAVID BLAINE, THE WORLD RECORD HOLDER
(17 MINUTES AND 4 SECONDS) FOR HOLDING HIS BREATH
UNDER WATER AFTER INHALING PURE OXYGEN.

How to Minimize Disappointment

The Secret of Magic

*Successful magicians never reveal the secrets of their illusions. But I can tell you this: Magicians **think about things differently** than everybody in the audience. And that can be a revelation for you as well.*

Have you ever asked somebody out on a date, but he or she says, "no," only to say "yes" to somebody you don't respect?

Have you ever had a supervisor pass you up for a promotion, but gives it to someone less qualified?

Or maybe someone who has been buying your service/product stops doing business with you and starts buying from a competitor who is a slime bucket?

How do you feel? Pretty disappointed? Not a good feeling.

When we relate with others, we expect them to relate back to us in similar fashion. If I give you a present on your birthday, I secretly hope that you'll remember mine and give me a surprise.

We expect people to be like us. To do things the way we do things. To react the same way we would react in a situation. But oftentimes, they don't. And seldom do they ever.

You will be less frustrated with people if you accept that people think differently than you.

It's OK to secretly think that the world would be perfect if everyone was like you; just don't expect it.

"I guess arcade tokens are better than no bonus at all."

How to Stand Out

Dangerous Illusions

Magicians, more than anything else, want to stand out. We want to be the show in town with unique effects found nowhere else. The effects that stand out most are the ones that are dangerous, such as escaping from a water chamber while straitjacketed upside down. That's the price to pay for standing out. That's what it takes for people to remember you.

It's vital for you to stand out from the crowd, both in your personal life and in business. Why would someone buy insurance from you over someone else? Why should somebody marry you instead of anybody else? Why should you get the job compared to others, who might have more experience or education than you?

You've got to stand out.

As a speaker and entertainer, I especially need to stand out from the crowd, both on stage and off. There are many ways to stand out, such as dressing nicely, being approachable, being friendly, anticipating others' needs, being funny, and being useful.

I want to share with you how I stand out with first impressions. When someone asks for my card, I take out my wallet and flames burst from the seams with my business card on fire. By the time I hand the card to the person, it's cooled off and people have just experienced the magic. They never forget it. Even years later, people tell me they still remember it.

Speaking of standing out, I know of a window cleaning service where, to stand out, the workers wear kilts. They get their photos taken and shared on social media, which generates buzz and business. I know the Cheese Ball Chick, a lady who brightens up strangers' day by giving cheeseballs through her unique cheeseball dispensing backpack. I know a speaker who has a red button sewn into all his shirts amongst all black buttons to remind him that, in order to make a difference in someone's life, he needs to be different. When people ask him about the red button, he tells them why, which encourages them to make a difference, too.

What are some ways you can stand out?

How to Connect with Anyone

Mindreading

Mindreading tricks are powerful. If someone could read your mind or thoughts and reveal that to you, would you be blown away? When a magician is about to connect with you on such an intimate level, it's a chemistry you'll remember for a while to come. What do you do to connect with others?

I've had people tell me, "I don't like small talk. I just want to have a conversation with people."

Well, I've got news for you. Small talk is extremely important because it's a conversation starter. It also helps the other party feel comfortable enough with you before engaging in more substantial conversations.

A few days ago, before I was scheduled to talk over the phone with a prospective client I had never met, I looked up his website, learned a bit about his industry, watched some of his online videos, and checked out his professional online profile. I was trying to find out things that stood out about him. Maybe things he was proud of, his hobbies, and his likes. Why? Well, to find common ground for small talk, of course.

When we did finally talk, we hit it off. I told him how much I enjoyed his website, how I had learned a few things from his videos, and I applauded him for all the people he has helped. Had I gone in cold, I wouldn't have had as much confidence, and the feel would have been different. After all the small talk, we decided to work together. Woo-hoo!

If you have opportunities to learn about people before you meet them, do it. It can be done through information online or ask mutual friends. Learn about what they do, what they're passionate about, and fun facts. It'll be a much more interesting conversation.

How to Small Talk

May I Have a Volunteer?
There is a reason why the magician has simple conversation with volunteers before asking them to pull out cash or to let him borrow a ring. Asking questions might seem trivial, but that's how trust and rapport are formed.

Here are some small talk conversation starters:

- What do you like to do for fun?

- What did you want to be when you were a kid?

- What did your parents want you to be?

- How did your parents come up with your name?

- That's a nice bracelet/necklace/hat. Is there a story behind it?

- Are you a [local sports team] fan?

The best connections are those in which you have areas in common. After all, if we like ourselves (and most of us do), then we think people who are like us are very cool.

"You're from my high school?" "You know Donald, too? How did you meet him?" "You're into photography, too?"

So my challenge to you is to find common interests. Do it with everyone around you. Do it before you engage in more intense conversation. If you do, you'll find over time that people will like you more, trust you more, and you'll be happier, too.

MAGICAL INSPIRATION

"*When people say you can't do it—that it's impossible—never lose hope. Just because they couldn't doesn't mean you can't.*"

—David Copperfield

Why You Should Be Vulnerable

The Table of Death

Perhaps the greatest commitment to your art is risking your very life to entertain the audience. The Table of Death requires the magician to be strapped down only to have above him spikes that will crush him once a fire burns through the rope supporting it. The magician is vulnerable and escapes just in time. I'm not suggesting that you (or anybody, really) attempt this illusion. I'm simply saying that the more vulnerable you are, the more people empathize with and relate with you.

Society tells us that we should be strong and not show weakness, but if you want to connect with people, you need to be vulnerable. No, I don't mean telling your whole life's sob story. And no, I don't mean spilling all your beans.

People like others who are real. People who honestly

say how they feel when it's easier to just sugarcoat and say everything is fine. It's very easy to talk about superficial things like movies, sports, good food, etc. And there is a place for small talk. It starts the relationship.

But after that, what *builds* the relationship is being vulnerable. Here are some examples:

- "Thanks for asking about my day. I generally enjoy work, but something happened today..."

- "Business has been kind of tough this year. I think it's because…"

- "I had a friend who was upset last night. I'm not sure what happened, but I'm trying to see how I can help her…"

©Glasbergen
glasbergen.com

"Do you ever think about other dogs while you're petting me?"

It's not necessary to share every detail, especially if you're just starting to be vulnerable. If a listener is interested, he or she will inquire further, like, "Was she mad when that happened?" or "Do you think it was your fault?"

Let the conversation naturally take its course.

When you share a vulnerability, it creates a connection. It makes you approachable. People know that you are human just like them. You have problems just like them. You have desires and disappointments just like them. It makes you more likable.

Plus, people will feel you trust them enough to share something personal, so they will usually reciprocate— either then, or at a later point, which will lead to more trust, which leads to more vulnerability, which leads to more trust.

12

Why You Should Ask for Favors

I Need Assistance

A magician will commonly ask for help from the audience. Perhaps it's help remembering a card or examining a magic apparatus to make sure there's nothing unusual about it. This makes volunteers feel helpful and needed, bonding them to the magician. It all starts with asking for a little help.

Connection is key to any relationship. One of the best ways is to ask for a favor.

Want to get to know a man or woman you like? Want to connect with a prospective client? Want to deepen your relationship with your kids? Friends? Strangers? Just ask for a favor.

I'm not saying to ask them to loan you $1,000,000, or hand-wash your car. No. I'm talking about simple favors that require interaction. It could be requesting feedback on a blog post you wrote. Or asking for a tip on what's the best way to surprise your significant other on your anniversary. Or soliciting suggestions on jokes you'll compile as your coworker's going-away present. Whatever.

By asking for a favor, you are inviting the other person into your life. You're saying "I respect you and value your opinion." Now, who doesn't want that?

This naturally segues to interaction, discussion, and perhaps even some future inside jokes. The person who did you the favor feels good for helping someone out.

If you make people feel good, they'll want to be around you more.

So, who are you going to ask for a favor from today?

How to Never Overlook an Opportunity

Three-Card Monte

You've seen it on the streets. I'm talking about the three-card monte. All you have to do to win is to follow that Queen of Hearts: Simple enough, right? In actuality, the opportunity is for the magician. He never passes the chance of making a few dollars off of every passerby.

Recently, a gentleman came into the lounge where I was and was asking another person questions about where a certain meeting was taking place. I obviously overheard the conversation, and there I had a decision to make. Should I help him or let him figure it out on his own?

I decided to tell him where the meeting was taking place. He was so appreciative he handed me his business card. Mind you, I didn't ask for it, nor did it cross my mind to ask for it. But since he did, I reciprocated by giving him my card. When he saw that I was a speaker, he asked me if I knew Zig Ziglar, one of the top speakers. Of course, I did. It so happens that he was a friend of Zig's and proceeded to share some wonderful stories about the man. Hearing those stories turned out to be the highlight of my week.

I learned some things from this experience.

- Always have business cards with you.

- Don't wait for people to ask you for a business card. Hand it to them.

- Never pass up an opportunity to meet someone.

- You never know who you might meet and where that may lead.

How to Deal with Toxic People

Snake-Charming

I once talked to a snake charmer. I found it incredible how someone can play with poisonous snakes and not get bitten. There's got to be a certain way to handle them. It's interesting that in life there are venomous people and it's a skill to know how to deal with them, lest you get bitten. Ouch!

You know who they are. When they enter a room, people feel uneasy and uncomfortable. You don't know if they are going to go ballistic or criticize you, perhaps even in front of others. Or perhaps they micromanage you, get under your skin, constantly try to manipulate you, or blame you for everything and credit you with nothing. They are just full of negative energy.

Here are some suggestions for dealing with a toxic person (which I am referring to as male only to avoid the cumbersome "he or she" or "he/she" thing):

- Have a talk and tell him exactly how it makes you feel when he says or does what upsets you. He may not be aware of how he impacts others.

- Reassure him that he is not a negative person (even though that might not be true), but that what he says and does can be perceived that way by you and others. Telling him straight up that he's toxic might only make him defensive, which doesn't help. You want to get him to be open to your suggestions. This communicates that you are trying to help, and it also gives him a reputation to live up to.

- Ask if you can offer solutions. It's always a good idea to get permission to suggest. He may be more open to ask for feedback. For example, "Instead of saying this (*give the example*) try saying it this way (*give example*)."

- Ask if he would be open to your letting him know of future incidents in which his words or actions might negatively affect you or others. This creates teachable moments. He may be more vigilant about watching his words and actions.

- Affirm every effort he makes to improve.

- If you've done all this and it's still not working, then tell him that you've given this a chance and might have to regretfully exit the relationship.

This shows that you really mean what you say. If he cares about keeping you around, he'll try to make an even greater effort. If not, then exit the relationship.

I know some people would never ever cut off toxic people in their lives, even though it is a viable option. Keep in mind that life is short, and toxic people can make your life even shorter. Does that sound harsh? Not at all. You see, if you are going to make this world a better place, you can't have people clipping your wings. You won't ever take off. You need to impact and influence the people around you, and can't afford people who drain you to the point where you can't give to others. Don't let them!

For the top seven most difficult types of people and how to deal with them download it here: www. itsnotmagicbook.com/toxic

15

MAGICAL INSPIRATION

---

*"Always know that there is
nothing between you and your
dream except you."*

—CRISS ANGEL

Why You Should Say "No" in Order to Say "Yes"

The Magic Guillotine

Have you ever seen the magic guillotine? Much of life parallels it. We have things or people in our lives that need to be cut off, but we don't. We know we ought to. Sometimes doing less is doing more.

Do you have more things to do than the time to do it? Swamped? Overworked? Then say "No"!

Of course, I'm speaking of when you have a choice. Be selective about with whom you hang out. Be selective about what you do with your time.

Can you outsource certain aspects of a project to someone else so you can focus on key tasks? It's perfectly OK to say "No" to opportunities or people. More doesn't necessarily mean better.

When you say "No" to something, you are essentially saying "Yes" to something else.

People who have a hard time saying "No" end up doing everything and meeting everybody. They tend to be spread so thin that they can't do too many things well. Their effectiveness is minimized. Their quality drops. They become a commodity. Don't be afraid of saying "No," because what you're really saying is "Yes" to yourself and higher priority tasks and people around you. It's your best way to contribute to society.

"SO DAD, WHAT MADE YOU DECIDE TO GET A TATTOO?"

Why You Should Be Nice

Why Are There No Rude Magicians?

Alright, I'll qualify that: It's possible there is at least one working rude magician out there and that he has somehow found the perfect balance between comedy, nastiness, and illusion. If there is, then my top hat is off to you, wherever you may be, the mythical Loch Ness Monster/Andrew "Dice" Clay of Illusionists. Otherwise, the point is that people who want to be entertained don't want to be abused. And neither do people just going about their everyday lives. Being nice will get you better results every time.

Recently I asked for a refund for a service that didn't deliver what it promised. It was supposed to help me find new clients. They had a risk-free, money-back guarantee. What I didn't realize was that I was two days beyond the scope of the guarantee, so I only got back some of my money. Disappointed, I asked for the rest back.

Now, I could have responded in one of two ways.

1. Got really mad and demanded my money back for a lousy service that wasted my time.

2. Be nice about it and just ask for the money back.

I chose the latter. Technically, it would have been fair for them to keep some of my money, but I didn't want to create a scene, vent how frustrated I was with the service, or how unhelpful it was to me. It wasn't necessary to be mean about it.

I simply admitted that I had miscalculated the timeframe during which I could ask for a refund, asked if she could talk to her boss and said if she could help me out, I would appreciate it.

A day later I got all my money back. Woo-hoo!

Whenever possible, it's always better to be nice.

Why Laughing Together is Important

Big Balloon, Little Head

One of my favorite tricks to perform is inflating a balloon until it's eight feet across. Next, I find a volunteer who I put inside of it. First his or her head goes in. Then the rest of the body, until all you see is the balloon. It's quite a sight. Not too many people have seen something quite like this so they laugh their heads off and we all have fun.

Some time ago, I was the host and Master of Ceremonies of a national real estate convention in town. A lady came up to me afterward and talked about how funny it was to see a friend of hers in a giant balloon. She kept laughing with me and we shared a special moment. That was touching to me— to be able to bring so much joy and laughter to her and the audience.

I've always believed that laughing is the apex of a great experience. It's so fun to laugh. There is release of stress and anticipation. When we look back at how much fun we have, people associate it with good memories and with you. Now that's connecting!

Do you know how to tell a joke? You don't have to be a professional comedian to tell a joke. In fact, I would say it's always a good idea to have a few jokes in your back pocket. That way, you can pull one out anytime you need to. Even cheesy or corny jokes would be better than having nothing.

With that, I want to share with you one of my favorite jokes with my spin on it. Feel free to use it.

Three guys are stuck on an island. They want to get off the island, but have no hope. One day a magic lamp floats up to the island. One of the guys picks it up, rubs it, and out comes a genie. The genie says, "OK. I've got three wishes. One for each of you." The first guy says, "I wish I were back at my job." The genie says, "Your wish has been granted." Poof. He's gone. The second guy says, "I wish I were back with my family." Poof. He's gone. The third guy says, "I really miss my two friends. I wish they were here with me."

For the one key comedy formula that you need to know in order to be funny download it here: www.itsnotmagicbook.com/funny

How to Make Somebody Else's Day

Pulling a Rabbit Out of a Hat

Perhaps there is no animal so associated with magic than a rabbit. Everyone asks, "So can you pull a rabbit out of a hat?" The sight of this furry critter never fails to get people "*Ooh*-ing" and "*Ahh*-ing." It feels so good to make someone's day.

Do you remember the last time someone complimented you in a meaningful way? Think about it. For some of us, it may have been a while. With our words, we can either give life or take life. We can either make someone's day or make them miserable.

When you express appreciation, don't just say, "Thanks" (although that can be a start). Be specific.

Here are some examples:

■ "Noah, you are such a thoughtful man. Thank you for offering to give Cindy a ride home tonight.

That's so appreciated. I wish more people were like you."

- "Juanita, you are such a brilliant woman. You were able to figure out the solution to that math problem just like that. I love how you can use your brain that way!"

Other ways to show appreciation can be giving a gift card, throwing a party, or perhaps offering tickets to a hot sporting event. The sky's the limit.

Obviously, it goes without saying that your compliments need to be genuine. At least they should *sound* genuine. If you're not good at sounding sincere keep working on it until it does.

So who are you going to appreciate today?

How to Give and Receive Feedback

Try This!

After a magic performance someone said, "You know that disappearing ketchup bottle trick you did? You might want to hold that out a little longer so people can more clearly see that it disappeared." I took the guy's advice and the next time I did the trick I heard much louder "Ooohs" and "Aaahs."

Just as in show business an accumulation of improvements from others' feedback can take what you are doing to the next level.

To help others improve, it's important to give feedback, but some ways to do it are better than others. Try these (and this time I'll refer to the hypothetical person as female):

- Compliment the person on something she did well. (If you can't find one thing she did well, chances are you might have too critical an attitude, and that can backfire.)

- Ask if she would be open to hearing feedback.

- Do it one-on-one. Most people prefer confidentiality.

- Give assurance that your only interest is to help the other person improve. This is not a chance for you to demoralize or belittle.

- Ask when a good time would be. Don't assume that now is the best time.

- Make sure your tone of voice is not condescending. Don't say things like, "I can't believe you didn't do this! How did you overlook this?"

- Use non-threatening words. Don't say, "Stop doing this. Do this." Instead, say something like, "Instead of doing this, have you thought about doing this?"

- Be clear. Usually this means being as specific as possible.

- Explain why you suggest what you have suggested. "I think if you did it this way, it would more clearly convey your idea to the group."

- Don't expect the person to accept your feedback. Keep in mind that your point of view may not be the best or only way to see things. If she doesn't change a thing, so be it.

- Thank the person for listening to your feedback.

- Make yourself available if she has further questions or comments.

Want to get the most out of your feedback from others? Try this!

- Be humble. You might be good at what you do, but it doesn't mean you don't have room to improve. Oftentimes, to get to the next level, you need others to point out your blind spots or help you.

- When someone is giving feedback and the time is not good, figure out a mutually agreeable time. It's hard to receive feedback when you're not in the mood or are tired.

- Don't write anybody off. Sometimes good feedback can come from people less educated, less accomplished, and less experienced than you. In other words, it can come from people you least expect.

- Don't be combative (e.g., "You suggest this, but you don't even know what you're talking about!").

- Listen to what others tell you. But that doesn't necessarily mean you should act on everything they tell you. You decide. Some feedback is more useful than other feedback.

- Don't take it personally. Some people might sound condescending or negative. Some don't use any tact. Try to overlook that as much as possible. Give people the benefit of the doubt; assume that they intend to help you.

- No matter what they say, whether or not it's helpful, say, "Thank you." Some people are taking a risk giving you feedback not knowing if you will receive it well or badly.

How Not to Take Things Personally

Floating Objects
It's not just people that magicians cause to levitate. Coins, cards, rings and fruit are common objects magicians will send seemingly floating into thin air. The lesson here: Rise above.

I know it's easier said than done. But when the man or woman of your dreams turns you down, you tend to take it personally.

Or when someone is not interested in your service/product you take it personally.

It's human nature. You think "What's wrong with me?" Sometimes there *is* something wrong with you. Maybe the person of your dreams doesn't think you're a responsible person. Or maybe your asking price for your service/product is too high. Or maybe you're not clearly explaining the benefits of choosing you.

There are times when you *should* take it personally. Maybe you have questionable character and integrity, are prone to rage, or have control issues. Or maybe people don't want your service/product because you don't offer good customer service or charge hidden fees. Let this be a lesson on how you can improve yourself.

But sometimes *it's not about you,* and in this case, it's not good to keep thinking about what's wrong with you. If you do, you'll take it personally. That can make you angry and frustrated. It can zap away at your confidence or take away that extra bounce in your step. In such a situation, reframe the circumstances

"My fleas don't pay any rent and they have loud parties that keep me awake all night. I want to have them evicted!"

and verbalize. For example, "It's their loss" or "I tried to help them. Oh well. <shrug your shoulders>."

There is a time to take things personally and a time not to.

How to Make People Feel Needed

Do You Find Anything Unusual About This?

*Many magic tricks call for the sincere assistance of
an audience member who is invited to come up to
the performance area and inspect an apparatus or
prop—the Chinese Rings, an empty box, a glass,
the top hat. Without the assurance to the rest of
the audience that everything is in order, the magic
wouldn't be nearly as impressive.*

When a friend asks you if you need water or
anything, always say "Yes," even if you don't really
need it. You see, she is hoping for the opportunity to
serve or help you in some way. When you say "No,"
immediately, she feels less important and unneeded.
It creates distance. The distance feels even greater
when it's something she really wants you to have.

For instance, she wants you to try the muffins that
were made from scratch. When you're offered a

muffin, instead of saying, "No, thanks!" just say, "Thanks. That smells amazing!" Even if you're full, accept one, take a little nibble, and say, "So, when are you going to start your own bakery?" Or maybe, "I'm going to save this until after my workout today. Thanks!" You'll make the other person feel good.

It's not about your needs. It's about making the other person feel needed, and that advances the relationship.

This is why it's important for people to have the opportunity to contribute. In a sports game, the players feel the elation of wins and the pain of losses much more than the ball boy. Why? Well, the players know that how they perform directly affects the results of the game. They know that their team needs them. They know that their roles are important. That's why they feel responsible for whatever happens on the field or the floor.

You might not be playing a sport, but other people around you would feel a lot better if you let them feel needed.

Why You Should Forgive Others

Sometimes Things Go Wrong

Magic isn't always fun and games. Although the longstanding myth that Houdini died while performing isn't true (he died of appendicitis), at least ten magicians have perished throughout recorded history doing dangerous tricks like bullet catch, escape tricks, and one—sadly—trying to amuse his own son when he fumbled an illusion that involved swallowing a rusty razor and actually did it for real. You can bet his son and wife, after they got over their shock, had to contend with some hurt—and forgiveness.

Who is someone who has offended you? Hurt you? Perhaps tried to tarnish your reputation? The thought of this person may send chills down your spine. Or maybe it makes you mad. Maybe you pretend you're over the incident (but you're not—not really).

Often we feel justified in holding a grudge or ill feelings toward someone. After all, that person deserves it for being such a jerk (or worse). You get what I mean. It's called inability to forgive.

But have you ever stopped to think that the primary person the inability to forgive actually hurts is *you*? It takes away any sense of well-being, levity, and freedom. You're the one with the mental anguish.

Now, forgiveness doesn't mean that you forget. You never forget what others do to you, especially evil things. And forgiveness doesn't mean you need to be friends again. That's up to you.

Forgiveness is simply you saying, "I'm not going to let this person ruin my enjoyment of life and the people around me. I will let go."

So who do you need to forgive today?

How to Accept that Not Everyone is Going To Like You

The Wringer

In this classic stage magic trick, the magician puts an assistant (or small animals, such as a rabbit or duck) through a large box with a set of rollers in the front of it. As the magician turns the crank, the assistant or animal emerges through the rollers, now apparently flat as a pancake. Later the magician may or may not restore the poor flattened beast to good-as-new status. The point? Accepting that not everybody in the world is going to like you is one way to keep yourself out of emotional rollers.

I'm a people person. I *love* hanging out with people. The good part is that I have so much fun. The bad part is that I want to please everybody. I want everyone to like me. And not everybody does. Can you relate with me?

For you, perhaps it's a family member who just rubs you the wrong way. Or a colleague who thinks you're stupid. Or perhaps it's an acquaintance who just doesn't get along with you.

There could be a gazillion trivial reasons why people might not like you. Maybe you remind them of somebody who hurt them. Maybe they don't like the way you dress. Or maybe they don't like your views or opinions. Now, assuming it's not your fault or a misunderstanding of sorts, you need to live with it.

Yup! You need to live with the thought that not everyone is going to like you.

If you don't learn to accept it, it'll eat you up. It'll dominate your thoughts. You might even get nightmares. Obviously, this is easier said than done, but it certainly can be done. It's a choice you make. Once you accept it, you will begin to experience peace of mind. You've done nothing wrong. You've done everything you can to make the situation better.

Accepting this means that you cease to care what this person thinks about you. With so much life ahead of you, you'll be glad you did.

25

MAGICAL INSPIRATION

"Your attitude, not your aptitude,

will determine your altitude."

—Zig Ziglar

Why It's Important to Be Down-to-Earth

There Are Only So Many Magic Tricks, But...

Every magician's show is unique, and it's not because every magician performs a set of unique illusions. What makes a magic show is his or her own rhythm, sequence, style, personality, stories, and "schtick." Some magicians are theatrical, some are dramatic, some are comedic. What makes magic shows successful—or not—is how magicians make the tricks their own.

I recently attended a speech training course. Everyone had to give a speech. At the very end, we would vote for who had given the best speech.

It was interesting that the person who was awarded best speech actually *didn't* give the *best* speech. Everyone gave a better speech than the winner, Mary Beth. So how in the world did she win?

Mary Beth had given a *terrible* speech. She did not
have stage presence. She did not speak coherently.
She did not use hand gestures well. But she did one
thing well. She emotionally connected with her
audience. Mary Beth's speech was on why she can't
give speeches.

She talked about her childhood, how her parents'
divorce made her emotionally unstable, how her
parents didn't even show up for her school graduation.
She talked about how she was surprised how terrified
she was trying to give her speech. The audience was
very moved by her speech in a way they weren't by
the other highly polished speakers' speeches.

It doesn't matter to people whether you went to an
Ivy League school or that you have an important
job. What matters is whether or not you're down-to-

"You're a vegetarian, I like rawhide bones. You like to drink with friends,
I like to drink from the toilet. You like to chase women, I like to
chase squirrels. Maybe we're not meant to be best friends."

earth. Mary Beth's audience could relate to her. Her audience felt her emotions. They saw Mary Beth as one of them. This is how you connect with people. You show them that you're just like them, both on stage and off.

How to Disagree Agreeably

A Magic Trick from the World of Improv Comedy

As a comic magician, I stand with feet in two worlds. One of the cardinal rules of improvisational comedy is the rule of "yes, and…" The basic premise is that when you're creating a scene with another participant, live and in the moment, you cannot negate what your partner just said with a negative word like "no" or "but." This has real-world implications, too.

There are many controversial topics that people are heated about. Some include illegal immigration, raising the minimum wage, racial profiling, and abortion, just to name a few.

I'm not saying that you should agree with someone else's view to keep the peace. You can still voice your opinion, but in a way where you don't invalidate or brush off the other person's view.

Let me explain. For instance, someone might say, "The minimum wage should be increased because people can't feed a family off of just a few dollars an hour." Someone with an opposing view will commonly retort, "I hear what you're saying, but…" or "That might be true; however,…"

The use of "but" or "however" negates and minimizes the validity of the person's view, which can be perceived as being disrespectful, thereby weakening the relationship.

Instead, try using a cushion. A cushion is a buffer that shows respect for the other person and for what he just said. Instead of using "but" or "however," use "and." For instance, "I hear what you're saying, and [*insert evidence to the contrary or your opinion here*]." (Instead of "and," a pause would do just as well.)

Try it. You'll have more civil discussions about controversial topics.

Why You Should Start a Conversation with a Compliment

Misdirection or Just Direction?

One of the controversies in the magic community is what to call the art of focusing an audience's attention where we want it. Some folks call it "misdirection." Others just call it "direction." If a magician wants you to focus on the ceiling or a top hat while the hocus-pocus is happening elsewhere, that's an act of direction. You can practice the same thing every time you meet someone new.

There's the standard "Hi. My name is Jack. What's yours?" way of starting a conversation, which works fine.

But if you really want to make a quicker, stronger connection and start off the relationship on a positive note, try complimenting the other person first with enthusiasm and zeal. You know, things like:

- You gotta tell me where you got that dress!

- I so dig your jacket. Can I have it? Just kidding.

- Wow. You've got a great smile. I could see it a whole block away.

- I love that perfume. So peachy!

- Look at that hair. You must be a movie star!

Chances are you'll be liked right away when you compliment someone. Try it!

Why You Should Count Your Blessings

Card Tricks

Of all the classic magic tricks, those that involve a deck of cards are some of the oldest. There are a number of magic tricks that involve counting cards; for a moment, though, I'd like to focus on counting something else.

Some years ago, I remember having Thanksgiving with some friends, and we did something I'd never done before. We went around the room to share about something we were thankful for. That really changed the mood. People became reflective. Some even started choking up. Here are some things people said:

- "I'm thankful for a roof over my head."

- "I give thanks for family and friends."

- "I'm thankful for food and a job."

Something powerful happens in our hearts when we pause to count our blessings. You see, in the course of life, what stands out are things that didn't work out as we expected. For example, maybe it was the sale that fell through, or that person who stabbed you in the back. Or was it the coworker from hell? This leads to bitterness and feeling slighted. Needless to say, in this state of mind, you're not going to be a bucket full of sunshine to those around you.

When you slow down to count your blessings, something changes in you. You realize that though life is tough, there is still much to be grateful for. No matter how hurt you are, there are people suffering far worse trials. You start to appreciate life and those people who are there for you, whom you've been taking for granted; usually they are the people closest to you. Your attitude starts to change. You start to bless those around you. And that starts to spread to others. If you want to change your community, count your blessings.

Don't wait until Thanksgiving. Start today.

MAGICAL INSPIRATION

"*Do you know what people want more than anything? They want to be missed. They want to be missed the day they don't show up. They want to be missed when they're gone.*"

—SETH GODIN

Why You Should Be Open to the Unexpected

Bill-in-Lemon

I love performing the bill-in-lemon trick. I borrow someone's $100 bill, only to make it disappear and reappear in the middle of a real lemon. Looking at a lemon, you would never guess there's money in it. But sometimes the unexpected lends a pleasant surprise.

Sometimes opportunity knocks on your door, but it's disguised. In 1997, two people approached Frank, a Ph.D engineering student, about joining a dozen others on a new business venture. Frank was raised in a home where education was valued, so he replied, "My parents would kill me if I quit my Ph.D. program," and politely declined.

Little did Frank know until years later that he had missed out on the opportunity of a lifetime. Had he joined the venture, he would have owned private jets and yachts today. The two people who had approached him were Larry Page and Sergey Brin, the founders of Google—one of the world's most valuable companies.

Obviously, everything is clearer in hindsight. But the point here is that Frank had a certain way of thinking, and this limited him. It kept him from exploring greater possibilities.

My question to you is, what kind of thinking do you have that may be limiting you? In work? In your personal relationships? In getting in shape? In eating right? In your goals?

It's worth pondering.

"The key to success is the one that locks the bathroom door. That's where I do my best thinking!"

How to Stay Motivated

The Best Show in Town

Magicians are egotistical. We want to have the best show in town, and that requires the best tricks and the best music to create the best experience. We're always wondering if our version of a particular effect is the best one. The motivation to be the best keeps us from being too comfortable. But how can motivation be sustained?

It's a strange sight at my gym. There's hardly anybody there. The gym guy tells me that come January, tons of people come in trying to work off overeating all those extra holiday meals. But as January turns to February and February to March, those who had the best of intentions don't even show up any more.

However, there are some people who are at the gym regularly. I see them. I wonder what makes them motivated to work out while others drop out? There can be tons of reasons. Maybe they are fitness nuts. Maybe they're avoiding future consequences of being out-of-shape. Whatever their motivation, it keeps them going.

I can see how easy it is to convince yourself not to go to the gym. Maybe it's dirty? Maybe you're too tired? Maybe you don't see immediate results? Maybe it's boring?

It only takes one good excuse to keep you from the gym. Conversely, it takes only one good reason to overcome all those excuses.

So, what's something you should be doing, but are making excuses not to? When are you going to do it?

How to Overcome the Fear of Failure

Sawing a Woman in Half

The most well-known illusion in magic is sawing a woman in half. Obviously, nobody dies, but one does wonder. If the magician does something wrong, could there be complications? In other words, there are risks. But just with anything in life, there are also risks with not taking risks. Failure is a possibility, but so is success.

For as long as I can remember, I passed up tons of opportunities because of fear. Job opportunities, educational opportunities, dating opportunities: you name it, all have disappeared. How about you? What have you passed up because of fear?

What is the biggest risk you've ever taken? Marrying someone? Putting tons of money on a single stock? Climbing a dangerous mountain?

For me, it's always been asking a woman I like out on a date. It might not seem like that big a thing, but tons of things go through my mind—things like, "What if she says no?" "Will things get awkward when we hang out with our mutual friends?" "If she turns me down, will it bruise my confidence?"

Potential romantic relationships are tricky. To pursue somebody you're interested in, you need to be vulnerable. You communicate how you feel about him or her. Then you wait. You hope the person reciprocates.

To give yourself an edge, it's important to reframe the situation. Let me explain.

You see, if you meet somebody who's great, you really have to be vulnerable and reach out. Your ego—your entire sense of self—is at stake!

Reframing the situation can give you a different perspective and even renewed confidence. So much confidence that you don't really care (well, of course, you secretly *will* care) if the person says "yes" or "no." The response is beside the point. For you, it's the preservation of your ego and believing that will give you the boost you need to ask him or her out. If you don't take risks, you are foregoing what life is about. If you shield yourself from pain, you'll have nothing to gain.

When you find yourself taking a risk and start to

doubt yourself, try reframing things. It might just give you the kick you need. The fear of failure is an opportunity-killer. But the more you just go ahead and do what you fear, the smaller that fear will be. Remember, the best salespeople have been rejected more than anyone else.

There needs to come a point when you get rejected so often that you don't care anymore. Then you become bold. But you have to pay your dues.

What is fear keeping you from doing? Ready to tackle it?

How to Further a Relationship

The Art of Stagecraft

A magic show is not a show *without the embellishments, lights, sound system, music, planned movements (blocking), scripting and all the other elements that create the mood and the setting for the tricks. These convey to the audience that the magician cares about his or her craft and helps them enter the right mood and frame of mind; it's an important part of furthering the relationship between audience and magician.*

Some time ago, I enlisted the help of a real estate agent to sell a property. I hardly ever heard from him. Days would turn into weeks, and weeks into months, and still the property was not sold. It was priced according to his recommendation (slightly under market rate). During this entire process, I had to constantly take the initiative to ask him how the sale was going. Not once did he call me to indicate that he was showing the property to prospective buyers. Not once did he tell me how he was marketing it online. Not once did he give me any updates. Eventually, I switched agents.

Now, was it possible that he was showing tons of prospective buyers the property and marketing the daylights out of it, but I was not aware of that? Yes. But because I never heard from him, that led me to think he didn't put much effort into it.

When someone asks you to run an errand or do a favor, it's fairly common for you to be asked, "How did it go?"

Most people will respond, "It was fine." This subtly implies that it didn't take much effort on your part. And because of this, the implication is that the person doesn't owe you much or need to feel much gratitude. The relationship doesn't get furthered.

Next time you're asked, try this: "I almost ran someone over trying to get to the store on time. But I knew how important it is to you that I get this done, so I skipped lunch. No, no, don't feel bad for me. I just had to ask everyone in that long line if I could cut in front of them because I was short on time. Thank goodness they were so nice. I'm just glad I could do this for you. You're such a good friend and I'm glad I can take care of you."

Of course I'm exaggerating, but you get the point.

When your family member, friend, or colleague understands the effort you put in, you will be greatly appreciated and the relationship is furthered. Try it!

35

MAGICAL INSPIRATION

"Comfort and prosperity have never enriched the world as much as adversity has."

—BILLY GRAHAM

Why You Should Never Respond When You're Angry

The Torture Chamber

A young woman steps into a box; she carries a string of balloons with her. At the top of the box, in the space over her head, is a group of long, sharp spikes. An audience member has inspected the spikes, and they are real, long, and sharp. So sharp that when the door is closed, and the magician starts to pound them in, the audience gasps as they hear the balloons popping. One. By. One. Surely they're also piercing the assistant's skull…

…Of course she steps out of the box miraculously OK. But each of those spikes increased the tension in the room. One. By. One.

I was having a long day. The last thing I needed was more bad news.

Jeff gave me bad news. He unloaded on me even though I'd nicely asked him not to do that anymore.

I was going to give him a piece of my mind.

I wrote out an entire e-mail expressing how upset I was. How I felt cornered. How unprofessional he had been.

I was about to hit *Send* when it dawned on me that my emotions were getting to me.

I held off.

When the heat had dissipated, I rewrote the entire e-mail, and the tone was completely different.

Jeff wrote back to apologize. Done.

Now, had I fired off the first version of the e-mail there would have been so much more tension in our relationship.

This leads to the point: Don't say a word when you're angry. That's when you *most* want to speak, but don't. That's when you *most* want to let the other person have a piece of your mind, but don't. That's when you *most* want to vent how fed up you are, but don't.

When you catch yourself angry, take a time out. Walk away from the situation. If you don't, you will regret what you say. It's a guarantee.

This is when you're most susceptible to calling someone else a regrettable name. This is when the other party gets hurt and perhaps hurts you back.

Wisdom is never spoken when a person is fuming hot. And neither is love. What is love? It is patient, kind, not envious, not conceited, not consumed with self-interest, not short-tempered. It doesn't hold others' pasts against them. It builds trust and is not only right, but does the right thing. It creates hope.

This is easier said than done, of course, but you can do it. Be the bigger person. Step away.

"LET'S FACE IT, YOU'RE BAD PARENTS.
YOU NEVER TAKE ME TO THE PARK OR THE ZOO..."

Why You Should Go the Extra Mile (or Kilometer)

Above and Beyond

I worked with a comedy script writer on jokes for my show. It was not easy coming up with original material, but my material will be unique to my audience. They won't hear these lines at any other show. The audience knows it and appreciates it. Every extra effort in whatever you do shows.

A hailstorm damaged the roof of my home. I called three roofers to have them come take a look and give me an estimate to repair the damage. All of them came to take a look. All of them were nice. All of them gave quotes that were comparable. Yet one stood out like crazy.

You see, all three roofers came to look at the damage, but only the third came back a second time, on his own initiative, to have a further look. He was wondering if perhaps there might be internal damage that a simple peripheral first look might not have uncovered. In this case, there was. We wouldn't have known it if he hadn't gone the extra mile. And because he did, he got the job over the other two.

Going a little extra for someone else sends the message that you care about the situation and that you value the relationship. This builds tremendous loyalty that will come back to you. It will grow your business or develop your reputation. Sound pretty awesome?

In whatever situation you're in, whether you're bidding for jobs, or pursuing that romantic partner, or raising a child, go the extra mile. It'll come back in your favor.

Why You Should Credit Others

There's No Such Thing as a Self-Made Person

There's a comedy mindreading duo act that my assistant and I perform. She's blindfolded, and I go around the audience raising borrowed objects into the air while she figures out what the object is. For example, I might say, "I'm holding something. Just guess. We don't have a lot of time!" "Time" is her cue that what I'm holding is a watch. This is just for laughs, of course. But I find that, as with any success, there are always people who made success possible for you. It's important to not forget them.

As you become more and more successful in life, keep in mind that you're not a self-made person. There were and are people around you who contributed to where you are today. There's a whole laundry list of individuals. Perhaps it's your family, who brought you into the world, raised you and/or gave you your first chance. Or maybe it was the teacher who believed in you when you doubted yourself. Or was it a coach who pushed you further than you thought you could go? For some, it's the people you hired to work on a project.

The point is, you are not where you are today solely because of you. People hate it when they've helped or served you in some way but you don't even bother to credit them. Sure, your determination or genius might have helped you get to where you are, but you still needed all those people around you from birth onward who made you *you*.

So the next time you give a speech or are in a social situation, don't forget to credit the whole army behind you (i.e. "I couldn't have done this without Ming, Juan, and Jane; these are the people who deserve to be recognized"). When you do, they'll want to support and help you even more and make you even greater. They'll feel valued and appreciated.

So, who are you going to give credit to today?

Why You Should Give More Than You Receive

Presto! Change-o!

If you want to get people's attention, turn someone's
$1 bill into a $5 bill. Want more attention? Turn that
into a $100 bill. Now give it away!

What? Give more than you receive? Yes.

That's the attitude you'll need to be a blessing to others.

When I was a kid, my favorite time of the year was Chinese New Year, because I would get red envelopes stuffed with money from my relatives and parents' friends. Whenever I got red envelopes, Mama would always open them up and see who gave how much. This helped her gauge how much she would give in cash to their kids. It wouldn't sit well with Mama if someone gave me $100 and she only gave $20 to their children.

So at a young age, I learned something about reciprocity—giving and receiving.

Though no one would admit it, we all keep a tally of what we give to others, both material and immaterial (time, energy, focus) and what we receive. We want things to be more or less equal (i.e. "If you get dinner tonight, then the next one's on me!" "Thank you for babysitting tonight. Please take this gift as a token of our appreciation."). We certainly don't want relationships in which we are constantly giving and getting little or nothing in return.

People are drawn to others who give to them. If you want to draw people to you, be that person. If you're ever in doubt where you stand with the scales of reciprocity with someone else, always err on the side of overgiving. You've got nothing to lose.

MAGICAL INSPIRATION

"Be a faucet, not a drain.
(And hang around all the
'faucets' you can!)"

—DAVID HIRA

Why You Shouldn't Compare Yourself to Others

Confession

I know I already said magicians are egocentric and all want to be the best. So I'm not going to open with a magic anecdote this time. I'm going to admit that sometimes, I even break my own rules.

It's only human. We compare ourselves with those around us on just about every level. You name it: attractiveness, wealth, success, relationships, intelligence, likability, material belongings, and more. This can only lead to two outcomes, neither of which is good.

You compare yourself with someone who has less than you and you may feel superior, arrogant, and prideful. You might think, "I'm so glad I'm not married to Jose," or "I'm just way smarter than Maria." This makes you hold your nose a bit higher, but it doesn't make you a better person. A better person will serve the needs of those around him, lifting them up. A better person will make everyone around him better. This approach doesn't do that.

The other option is to compare yourself with someone who has more than you, and that leads you to feeling jealous, envious, or sorry for yourself. You'll complain, "Why was I born into such a family?" or "Why can't I be as talented as Jerry?" or "If only I can be pretty like Sarah…" This leads to insecurity, lack of confidence, and wanting others to fail. Likewise, in this example, you still won't be interested in pushing others up. It won't make you a better person.

The solution is to make a choice to be comfortable with being you. I'm not saying that if you're out-of-shape, that you should not be bothered by that. Nor am I saying that you shouldn't be striving to sharpen

©Glasbergen
glasbergen.com

**"Actually, I'm 60% leaner than you.
I'm made from turkey!"**

your skills or opportunities. I'm saying you have a unique role in history. You're the only one who can touch and influence those around you in your special way. Just be you.

Why You Should Try to Get Rejected as Much as Possible

If at First You Don't Succeed…

Behind any good trick is lots of practice. In fact, a five-minute act on stage could represent thousands of hours of practice and refinement. And within those many hours were countless times where something didn't go right or something failed. But that's part of paying your dues. There's no shortcut. It's also true in life. You can't have success without cost.

Nobody likes being rejected. It hurts. It stings. And worse yet, it's something you'll remember for a long time to come. Just think of the time when you wanted a job really badly, only to be rejected. Or maybe a school rejected your admission application. Or maybe your crush rejected your hopes of having a future together.

To minimize rejection, people play it safe. You find the safe job. You dismiss aspirations that require risks. You put yourself in positions in which people can't really reject you.

I've got news for you. If you don't get rejected much, it means you are not giving yourself a chance to be more. It means that you are likely not reaching your potential. It means you're settling in life when you could be doing much better.

When Walt Disney started off as an aspiring artist, nobody gave him a chance. He was a decent artist; certainly not the best in the world or anywhere close, but he kept trying. Through rejection after rejection, he kept plowing ahead until he got his break. Had he let these rejections set him back, Disneyland would not exist today.

After J.K. Rowling wrote Harry Potter, not one, not two, not six, but *twelve* publishers rejected it. Rowling could have just given up, but she kept at it. She eventually got her big break, and the rest was history. In fact, you'll even find The Wizarding World of Harry Potter attraction at Universal Studios theme parks in Hollywood and Orlando.

You might be saying, "Well, I'm not Disney or Rowling." You're right! You are you. You're going to leave your mark in the world, but to do that you need to start piling up the rejections, which means getting out there. Or if you really want to play it safe, you can hide in your closet the rest of your life. No one's going to reject you. But is that what you really want?

Those who get rejected the most achieve the most. Ready to get rejected?

Why You Should Be the First to Apologize

The Magician in Trouble

The audience expects the magician to have everything worked out. But sometimes magicians mess up on purpose. It's called "Magician in Trouble." For instance, the magician asks you to name your card. You say, "Eight of Hearts," and he pulls out the King of Diamonds. He apologizes profusely. But somehow, some way, he makes it right. In life, apologies are harder to come by, but when it happens, it's a good thing.

Whenever something goes wrong, it's so easy to point the finger at someone else. Nobody wants to look bad, so when we blame someone else it makes us feel better. But often this makes things worse.

Let's say you are responsible for organizing a breakfast meeting. Unfortunately, Rick, the person you put in charge of bringing the bagels, forgets. Now, you can blame Rick all you want in front of other employees, but what message are you communicating to them when you're fuming mad at Rick? Does it inspire others to work harder for you? Does it create fear that what happened to Rick can happen to them one day? Does it promote a healthy, positive workplace culture?

The employees will think you are a mean-spirited, hard-to-work-with boss. Of course, you might have the *right* not to be blamed for the food not showing up, but we're talking about how you'll be perceived, which is hard to undo.

Instead, wouldn't a better response be, "Guys, I'm so sorry the bagels haven't arrived yet. Let me go check on it." In other words, take the hit. This response tells everybody that you're taking full responsibility for this and that you're not going to chastise one of their own in front of them.

This will spare Rick public humiliation, for which he will be thankful, and he'll make sure not to forget about it next time, since you cut him some slack. Rick will have a more favorable impression of you since you took one for the team when he was responsible. The employees won't have a negative impression of you blaming everyone else for shortcomings. They'll like you even more. In fact, they'll respect you for owning up.

People aren't expecting perfection from you. When things don't go the way they're supposed to, they just want someone to be brave enough to say "This one's on me. Sorry." That's why it's a good idea to take the fall and race to apologize first.

Why You Should Stand Up for Those Who Can't Stand Up for Themselves

---

Sword Swallowing

Sword swallowing is not for the timid. A centimeter here or there can spell disaster. In other words, don't do this challenging feat at home. Speaking of challenges, there are people who face them and get harassed by others. What you do next will be telling.

When I think about middle school, I cringe because I didn't stand up when I should have. I had a blind friend named Paul who was teased and bullied for his blindness. Obviously, he wasn't in a position to fight. Sadly, I witnessed this several times and didn't do anything about it. I think it was because I was afraid that the bullies would beat me up or make my life miserable. I was more concerned about my own well-being than Paul's.

In high school, I had a friend named Steve who was bullied for his odd behavior. He was a nice kid. He never threatened anyone. He was just a little odd, and yet again, I was a witness to the bullying and did nothing. I didn't want to be called a tattle-tale. I didn't want to be labeled a snitch. I was more concerned with my social reputation than with Steve's well-being.

Looking back at my life, there were probably other times when I didn't stand up for those who couldn't stand up for themselves. I sometimes justify my glossing over the situation, thinking, "Well, it's none of my business" or "It's not like they were picking on me." But a real friend will stand up for his friends. He will do whatever he can to make things right.

Perhaps for you it's someone at your workplace. Your boss or colleagues are ganging up on somebody unfairly. You could stand up for him or her, but then maybe everyone will hate you. Or maybe you might get fired. Will you stand up?

Bullying doesn't end in school. It's everywhere around us. I've failed Paul and Steve. I don't plan to fail again. Who is it in your community or workplace who is being bullied? Scorned? Pushed down? Treated unfairly? Will you let it continue? Will you just turn the blind eye and make an excuse? Or will you stand up for them?

The choice is yours.

MAGICAL INSPIRATION

"*Sometimes me think, 'What is a friend?' and then me say, 'Friend is someone to share the last cookie with.'*"

—Cookie Monster

Why You Shouldn't Let Your Past Hold Up Your Future

The Hand You Are Dealt
"No matter what hand you're dealt, don't let anyone tell you you can't play."

—RICHARD TURNER, ACADEMY OF MAGICAL ARTS MAGICIAN OF THE YEAR.
(WHAT YOU MIGHT NOT KNOW IS THAT HE'S BLIND.)

My first business right out of college was a disaster. I started an educational service helping high schoolers test prep and write personal statements for college entry. I had zero idea how to market and grow my business so I bought a mailing list for $20,000 and sent out thousands of postcards to homes with teenagers. Then I waited by the phone. When it finally rang, the caller asked "Do you mind removing me from the mailing list?" I did not receive another phone call. Talk about depressing. $20,000 right down the drain.

This was not my only failure. I had more. I tried starting other types of businesses and failed at them also. Pretty much anything I did was a disaster. It was not easy to keep trying because my peers were wondering why I was changing my job so frequently. My parents were embarrassed to mention where my career was going to their friends whose kids were successful in their careers. There was certainly pressure. But I couldn't let my disappointments stop me from figuring out exactly what I should do with my life. I could have stopped trying and just got a safer job where I knew I would get paid every two weeks, but something didn't seem right about that.

I kept trying to figure out my calling and who I was. Then a few years ago something amazing happened. I went to a conference in Seattle where an amateur magician named Rasy was showing a card trick, turning a regular deck of cards into all aces. I was blown away. At that moment I felt like a different person. I knew then and there that magic would be my life, at least a huge part of it. That encounter eventually led to my performing for Fortune 500 companies, celebrities, and countless very interesting people I otherwise wouldn't have met. And that led to keynote speaking, which led to writing books, like the one you're reading now.

All this was possible only because I kept trying and looking for what I was supposed to do in life. I didn't let my past failures hold up my future.

What is it about your past that's holding you up from accomplishing more in the future? Perhaps like me you had setbacks. Maybe you never felt like you accomplished anything in the eyes of your parents or peers? Maybe some people bullied or called you names? Maybe you make excuses for yourself because of a disability? Maybe you've made some poor decisions that still affect you today? Or maybe it's this or that. Whatever excuse it is, just remember:

Your past doesn't have to be your future.

"I have a 'delete' button tattooed on my forehead.
It helps me forget about my day."

Why You Should Help Those Who Can Never Repay You

Magically Appearing Coins

*Have you ever had a magician pull a coin out
from behind your ear? Where did that come from?
It's almost as if money can appear out of thin air.
Wouldn't it be awesome to be able to do that in life?
You would be able to help so many people—even those
who can't really pay you back.*

People work on the principle of reciprocity. (Most people, at least.) You help me. I'll help you. You scratch my back and I'll scratch yours. We usually don't keep those who reciprocate very little to none as friends for too long. But what about those who are not in a position to return the favor? Not because they don't want to, but they just can't. This may include people who are poor, chronically sick, mentally traumatized, and disabled—perhaps thought of as the less fortunate.

If you realize that you are among the more fortunate in society, and that many people helped and served you, you simply cannot turn away from sharing your abundance with others. In fact, when you give to others, it's you who will receive.

Just as an example, giving a cup of water or a meal or a blanket to a homeless person does something to your being. Helping people who are trafficked out of bondage does something to your being. Providing an opportunity for an ex-felon to restart his life does something to your being. You become more in touch with the real world because of it. You become more compassionate. You become a better person. You're reminded that life is not measured in how many nice cars you own or how many awards you have or your net worth, but how many lives you touch, particularly those who cannot repay you.

So lend a hand to someone who cannot repay you. It's the best thing you can do…for yourself.

How to Create a Magical Reputation

Levitation Tricks

If you've seen a woman levitating, chances are a magician's in the room. You're thinking, "How is she floating? Is there an invisible wire? How is that possible?" In just a few moments, the woman comes back down to earth. Because it's so amazing, the magician will develop a reputation, something that precedes him wherever he goes. What's your reputation?

One day I was talking to the CEO/President of Holiday Inn as I was driving him to his hotel.

Just like I do with any successful person, I asked, "What are the keys to your success?"

He said, "Anticipating needs."

I've thought about this concept and wondered:

■ How cool is it when a server fills your glass with water without your asking?

■ How thoughtful would it be for someone to offer to help you move furniture up those stairs without your asking?

■ How nice would it be if the hotel staff offered you a late checkout without your asking?

In order to anticipate needs, you need to constantly ask, "What are the needs of people around me?"

If you're thoughtful, you'll figure it out. Just put yourself in someone else's shoes.

■ If you were a schoolkid about to go back to school, what would you want? A new backpack? Cool folders? New shoes?

■ If you were the parent of a young toddler flying on a plane, what would you want? Some crayons? A coloring sheet? Some Gummi Worms?

■ If you were a teacher, what would you want? Markers? Prizes to motivate kids? An end-of-the-year magic show for your class?

■ If you were a new car salesman, what would you want? Videos on how to close a sale? A new tie?

If you put yourself in other people's shoes, before long, you'll be in high demand. And if you're in the service industry, you'll create a reputation for outstanding customer service.

So whose shoes are you going to put yourself in? Trust me—it works like magic.

Why You Should Be Discontent

Quick-Change

Quick-change magicians change from one outfit to another in the blink of an eye. Don't like that outfit? Poof. Here's a new one! These changes happen quickly, similar to life. If you grow too content with where you are, eventually you'll be left behind.

Kodak was a company that controlled the film industry. They were making millions every year and didn't have any significant competitors. Then along came digital cameras. For the first time, a person could capture a photo without film.

Kodak wasn't worried. They were happy where they were and reasoned that digital photos still weren't as high quality as film and that people wouldn't ditch film for digital prints.

Then as digital technology improved to a point where it was on par with film quality, it was too late. People started switching in droves to digital and it was just a matter of time before Kodak went out of business.

Here's another story about two fabled companies: Yahoo and Google. Google learned a valuable lesson from Yahoo, which was once the most visited website in the world, offering e-mail, news, games, etc. In its heyday, Yahoo was so market-dominant that advertisers were dumping tons of money on them in advertising. Yahoo was so market dominant that they were making tons of money in advertising. Long story short, other competitors started competing effectively against them and lured their customers away. Their stock has plummeted and has never come close to where it once was.

Google, the current market leader, started off as a search engine service but knew that they couldn't be content to rest there, lest they drop like Yahoo. Contentment will lead to a lack of innovation and improvement, which allows competitors to step in. Google expanded into new territory, aiming to provide the best services available, offering e-mail, videos (YouTube), maps, writing tools, access to books, wireless internet-connected glasses, driverless cars, etc. Their lack of contentment has kept Google one of the world's most valuable companies.

The lesson is this. If you're content with where you are, you won't push for progress, and it might be a matter of time before you start regressing. Don't be content with anything. Whether you're a mother, father, son, daughter, worker, or employer, there is room to improve.

MAGICAL INSPIRATION

"The more you like yourself, the less you are like anyone else, which makes you unique."

—WALT DISNEY

Why You Need a Coach

Learning Magic

If you want to find out how a common magic trick is done, you can search online, but the most guarded secrets in magic are not there, nor are they in books. They're passed down from one magician to another, apprentice-style. Just as a master can help a student achieve his potential in magic, so likewise a mentor can help you in a certain aspect of life. Do you have such a person?

I have had the privilege of meeting some of the top athletes in the world, including Steve Young (a Super Bowl champion and Super Bowl MVP), Joe Montana and Jerry Rice (four Super Bowls each), and Mike Tyson (Heavyweight Champion of World). None of them would have been able to accomplish what they did without coaches.

Sports coaches help with various things. Some help athletes bulk up and become stronger. Some help build mental toughness. Some impart strategy. And some inspire them to greatness.

Maybe you're not an athlete, but it's no different, whatever field or area you are in. Coaches are essential for progress in both your personal and professional life.

Let's say you're a parent. A good coach will impart wisdom on how to raise your kids, what works and what doesn't, and how to discipline. If you're in business, a good coach will help you be accountable on sales goals, staying focused, and negotiating deals.

Could you do these things without help? Yes, but probably not as well. A good coach will cut your learning curve and help you hit the ground running.

I've had various coaches in my life. I've had comedy coaches who taught me the structure of writing good jokes. I've had spiritual coaches who impressed on me the importance of putting others first and serving people's needs. I've had business coaches who gave me tips on attracting prospective customers. Because of their help, I'm much further ahead than where I would have been on my own.

Having a coach is one of the best investments you can make in yourself.

What area do you need help with today?

How to Minimize Regret at the End of Your Life

The Bullet Catch—And The Magicians Who Didn't

There have been a handful of magicians who have died performing the bullet catch. Done successfully, someone fires a bullet at the magician, only to have him catch it between his teeth. When I attempt this stunt, I look into the barrel of the gun and my life flashes before me. I know everything will be fine, but I can't help thinking, "Did I do life right?" Ever ask yourself this?

At the end of your life, if you're like most people, you'll have regrets. Here are a few of the top regrets, according to the article "The 25 Biggest Regrets in Life. What Are Yours?" in *Forbes* magazine:

■ Choosing the practical job over the one I really wanted

- Not spending more time with the kids

- Not taking care of my health when I had the chance

- Not having the courage to get up and talk at a funeral or important event

- Worrying about what others thought about me

- Not having enough confidence in myself

- Living the life my parents wanted me to live instead of the one I wanted to

- Not being happier more

- Taking life too seriously

- Not going on more trips with the family/friends

- Letting my marriage break down

- Not asking that woman/man out

- Not trusting that voice in the back of my head more

- Working so much at the expense of family and friendships

- Not standing up to bullies in school and in life

- Not staying in touch with some good friends from my childhood and my youth

So, what do you need to do today to minimize future regrets?

"I try to live each day as if it were my last."

APPENDICES

Resources

Here's a list of wonderful authors I've enjoyed reading insights from:

Alessandra, Tony	GOD (The Bible)
Altucher, James	Godin, Seth
Ariely, Dan	Goldsmith, Marshall
Baer, Jay	Gordon, Jon
Beckstrom, Rod	Harnish, Verne
Berger, Jonah	Hayzlett, Jeffrey
Blanchard, Ken	LaCroix, Darren
Brafman, Ori	LeBlanc, Mark
Brafman, Ron	Lencioni, Patrick
Brown, Les	Michelli, Joseph
Burger, Jonah	Nomura, Catherine
Carnegie, Dale	Pincott, Jena
Carter, Judy	Pink, Daniel
Cialdini, Robert	Scott, David Meerman
David, Tim	Sherren, Joseph
Davis, Andrew	Slim, Pamela
DeVries, Henry	Tate, Ed
Dijulius III, John R.	Tracy, Brian
DiSalvo, David	Watkins, Alexandra
Fine, Debra	Westergaard, Nick
Fripp, Patricia	Valentine, Craig
Gard, Tim	Ziglar, Zig

Applause

I wish to thank the following for their insights and contributions to this book. In no particular order: Jesus, Ben and Angelia Hao, Barry Friedman, Henry DeVries, Vikki DeVries, Devin DeVries, Mark LeBlanc, Brian and Allison Campbell, Denise Montgomery, Gareth and Linda Seeto, Denise Wozniak, Elaine Lung, Skip Weisman, Robert Iyer, Tim Wilson, Dave Nothhelfer, David Fritzlen, Barry Friedman, David Hira, Joni McPherson, Jamey French, Marisa Shadrick, Derek Oullette, Vivian Gee, Julie Reuter Sunne, Dale Callahan, Sam and Helen Livingston, Lara Helmling, Jason Goudy, Bill McConnell, Patrick Mulligan, Bam Bam, and Beano.

About the Author

Born and raised in San Francisco, Mike Toy is a corporate trainer, entertainer, and keynote speaker for international conferences and Fortune 500 companies. His clients include Google, eBay, and Citibank. For fun, he enjoys sightseeing, beach volleyball, and watching comedies. A fun-loving, full-of-real-world-wisdom kid at heart, Mike has implemented his insights in all his endeavors with astounding results. He can do the same for you!

To receive Mike's e-newsletters visit:
www.itsnotmagicbook.com

To inquire about Mike's availability for speaking or training contact him at: www.mikejtoy.com

Magical Quotes to Make Your Day

Ambition

Give all you can give, and then give a little more.

You'll go as far in life as your imagination.

Pursue the dreams that pursue you.

Don't do tomorrow what you can do today.

Don't wait for all the ducks to line up. Line them up yourself.

If you don't swing for the fences, you'll never hit a home run.

The best way to climb a mountain is to not look down.

Use naysayers to motivate you.

No great work has ever been achieved in one's comfort zone.

Attitude

Your past wounds don't define who you are.

There is no competition if what you do is unique.

There's always room for improvement.

Don't let your past hold up your future.

It's never too late to make the most of your life.

If you please everyone, you will no longer be you.

Never forget the people who made you *you*.

Life is full of second chances. We call it *tomorrow*.

Discipline sustains when motivation wanes.

What you think about is who you become.

Let go of every thought that doesn't serve you.

Good enough is not good enough.

The greater the obstacle the greater the satisfaction.

Discontentment leads to innovation.

Don't just be the best choice. Be the only choice.

Challenges

The hard path is often the right path.

The stars will only show in the dark times of life.

The hardest step in following your dreams is the first one.

Just because it's hard doesn't mean the door is closed.

Trials in life can make you either better or worse. You choose.

If you're afraid of something, chances are you ought to do it.

Discipline is doing what you don't feel like doing.

When a door closes, think of another way in.

Mastery requires much failure.

Closed doors here mean open doors elsewhere.

Obstacles are stepping stones to success.

Use your setbacks to set up success.

Character

Own your mistakes. People will respect you for that.

Be a better person than you were yesterday.

Just because everyone does it doesn't mean you should.

A wise person listens to what he doesn't want to hear.

Make your day by making someone else's.

Wake up each day determined to love people.

How people remember you depends on how much you care.

Be the reason someone smiles.

It's impossible to give more than you receive.

How you treat those who can never repay is who you really are.

Don't care too much what others think about you.

If you please everyone, you please no one.

Freedom is the moment you decide to be yourself.

Happiness

Thankfulness is the secret to happiness.

Find something beautiful to look at each day.

Happiness is not what happens to you. It's a choice you make.

Enjoy the little moments of each day.

Don't worry about tomorrow. Just take care of today.

There is always something to be thankful for.

Do something today you'll be thankful for years from now.

The more gratitude you express, the more gratitude you'll have.

Rainbows follow storms to tell you it's going to be all right.

When life deals you bad cards, bluff.

Leadership

Become the leader people want to follow.

A true leader pulls others up.

There's a time to follow and there's a time to lead.

Leaders are seldom understood by people.

Vision is seeing possibilities when others don't.

Know when to follow the rules and when to break them.

Courage is standing for right even when no one else does.

Expect much from those around you, but expect even more from yourself.

The right person on the right team leads to the right results.

People will gladly follow you if they know you have their best interests at heart.

People

Make it easy for others to say hello to you, but hard to say goodbye.

If you want to make this world a better place, it starts with you.

How you make people feel is how you'll be remembered.

Forgiving someone is primarily for your own benefit.

It's better to be alone than to be with bad company.

You can learn something from everyone.

After you forgive everyone, don't forget to forgive yourself.

Nothing wonderful is accomplished without a team.

Allow others to push you further than you would go on your own.

Be the first to say "Hello!" There's no knowing where that will lead.

Success

Don't let success define you. You define it.

Envisioning success is half the battle.

The heights you'll soar to depend on your determination.

A small step in the right direction is a big step.

Those who are least satisfied with life accomplish the most.

Success is not in how much you make, but how many lives you touch.

Listen closely to what life teaches.

Don't be so busy you miss opportunities.

The best thing and the right thing are the same thing.

Change is the succession of good ideas.

Don't let worrying take you away from the present.

Success is taking one more step than everyone else.

Values

Don't get caught up accumulating things you can't take to the grave.

Focus on what's most important first.

Remember what really matters.

Take time to be quiet each day.

The intangibles are often more important than the tangibles.

Don't pass up opportunities to invest in yourself.

If your success only benefits you, you've missed the point.

Values are taught, not caught.

People are more important than things.

"Run around the house with a sock in your
mouth for five minutes a day. Trust me,
it will put you in a better mood."